CU01509963

Original title:
Umbral Calls Among the Fae Yoke

Author: Kätriin Kaldaru
ISBN HARDBACK: 978-1-80563-029-6
ISBN PAPERBACK: 978-1-80564-550-4

## Beneath the Gloom of Twilight Wings

Beneath the gloom of twilight wings,
Shadows dance and softly sing.
Whispers linger in the air,
Secrets spoken, tales of fare.

Stars emerge, a silver glow,
Drawing forth the dreams we sow.
In the hush, we find our place,
Wandering through this moonlit space.

Echoes of the night unfold,
Stories whispered, brave and bold.
Creatures of the dark arise,
Guided by the starlit skies.

Crickets chirp a soft refrain,
Pulsing like a gentle vein.
Nature's lullaby calls low,
To the heart's true path we go.

As the night begins to wane,
Light of dawn will break the chain.
Yet in dreams, we shall remain,
Beneath the gloom, our souls sustain.

## Enchantment Beneath the Veil

In the forest, shadows creep,
Where the moonlit secrets sleep.
Veils of mist entwine with fate,
Stirring magic, soft and weight.

Wandering through enchanted trees,
Stories carried by the breeze.
Softly sings the lark at dawn,
Awakening the world reborn.

Petals shimmer, glinting bright,
Weaving spells in morning light.
Glances shared in whispered tones,
This enchantment seems like home.

Laughter dances on the wind,
In this realm, our hearts rescind.
Time suspends in hues so fair,
Breathless, lost in purest air.

Beneath the veil, old legends breathe,
Silken threads that weaves and wreathe.
In this magic, ever near,
We find our truth, we conquer fear.

# The Call of Elusive Phantoms

In the twilight's gentle haze,
Phantoms call in whispered ways.
Voices echo through the night,
Guiding hearts toward the light.

Through the mist, they weave and twirl,
Elusive figures, visions swirl.
Haunting melodies they play,
Tempting souls to drift away.

Gather 'round, dear friends of night,
Follow phantoms, chase the light.
In the dance of shadows' grace,
Find enchantment in their face.

With each step, the world transforms,
Bringing forth the mystic forms.
In divinity, we shall bask,
Every question, every task.

So heed the call, let spirits soar,
Open wide the hidden door.
For with phantoms, journeys blend,
In the echoes, time transcends.

# Mystic Encounters in the Faerie Wood

In the woods where faeries play,
Magic twinkles night and day.
Every leaf, a tale unfolds,
In their whispers, promise holds.

Dancing light beneath the trees,
Carried softly by the breeze.
Every glimmer, every spark,
Guides the weary through the dark.

Flickering, the shadows shift,
With each heartbeat, spirits lift.
Lost in wonder, hearts are free,
Drifting in this reverie.

Ancient runes upon the ground,
In their beauty, truth is found.
In this realm, we feel the pull,
Of the faerie's gentle lull.

So wander deep, let senses tingle,
In the faerie wood, we mingle.
With each step, a bond will grow,
In this magic, we will know.

# Whispers of the Twilight Cascade

In the hush of dusk, where shadows play,
Echoes of dreams drift softly away.
Ripples of magic on water's face,
Whispers entwined in a twilight embrace.

Stars awaken, their flickers ignite,
Glimmers of hope in the velvet night.
Crickets serenade, a symphonic tune,
As the world hums softly, beneath the moon.

Moss-covered stones in a twilight glen,
Tell tales of wonders, of where they've been.
Glistening dew clings to leaves so green,
In secrets held close, where few have seen.

Beneath the boughs where the fireflies dance,
Magic reveals in a fleeting glance.
A heartbeat lingers, like time stood still,
In the quiet moments, dreams softly spill.

With each breath taken, a spell is spun,
Under the arch of the setting sun.
So listen closely, let your heart glide,
In the twilight cascade, let wonder abide.

## Echoes Beneath the Fairy Lights

In the hush of night, where dreams take flight,
Flickering orbs, a whimsical sight.
Beneath the canopies of emerald green,
Myriad stories in shadows are seen.

Each whispering leaf sings of delight,
Amidst twinkling stars that hold the night.
Dancing in circles, the fairies weave,
Threads of enchantment that never deceive.

They gather 'round in the soft, silver glow,
Casting their spells in a delicate flow.
Laughter like music floats through the air,
Echoes of joy, a sweet, fleeting fair.

Time tread softly on this sacred ground,
Where mysteries lie and magic is found.
In moonlit meadows, wishes take flight,
Carried away on the wings of the night.

So venture forth, let your spirit ignite,
Hold dear the moment, a treasure so bright.
For in the silence, while hearts intertwine,
Whispers of dreams are forever divine.

# The Secrets of Hallowed Hollows

In the depths where shadows play,
Whispers stir at close of day.
Ancient trees with boughs that quake,
Guard their secrets for the brave to take.

Moonlight dances on the ground,
In this realm where dreams abound.
Echoes of a long-lost song,
Beckon souls to wander along.

Riddles wrapped in twilight's shroud,
Voices call from beyond the crowd.
Courage found in the darkest place,
Brings the wanderer to the chase.

Through the mist, a figure stands,
Guiding paths with unseen hands.
In the hollows, truths unfold,
Stories whispered, brave and bold.

As the night begins to fade,
Secrets linger, never paid.
For those who seek with open heart,
Hallowed hollows play their part.

# When Shadows Dwell in Sylvan Dreams

Where the ancient trees entwine,
Whispers weave in dreams divine.
Shadows dance beneath the eaves,
Telling tales the heart believes.

Silvery mists across the ground,
In the stillness, magic found.
Twilight beckons, soft and sweet,
As night creatures softly greet.

Stars above begin to gleam,
Cradling every fleeting dream.
In this realm of whispered fate,
Time shall weave a silver gate.

Starlit paths of ethereal light,
Guide the soul through endless night.
In the shadows, hope does bloom,
Filling hearts with sweet perfume.

When shadows dwell, do not fear,
For the night brings wisdom near.
In sylvan dreams, where spirits blend,
Magic lies beyond each bend.

# A Cascade of Light in the Woods of Gloom

In the woods where shadows creep,
Silent secrets lie in sleep.
Yet amid the darkness' hold,
A cascade of light, bright and bold.

Flickering flames of will-o'-the-wisp,
Guide the lost with a gentle lisp.
Through the gloom, they weave and swirl,
An enchanted path begins to unfurl.

Moonlit glades kiss the earth,
Whispers of forgotten mirth.
With every step, the shadows dance,
Inviting those who dare to chance.

And though the night may seem so deep,
A promise in the silence keeps.
For in gloom, as fears subside,
Light will shine and dreams abide.

A cascade brilliant in the night,
Follows those who seek the light.
In the woods, both brave and free,
Hope is found, eternally.

# The Language of the Creep of Vines

In gardens lush where shadows twine,
There lies a tale, the creep of vines.
Silent whispers tell the tale,
Of creeping roots that never fail.

With every twist, a secret shared,
Underneath the soil, unscared.
The language of the earth below,
Speaks of life in ebb and flow.

Tendrils reach for light above,
In tangled paths, they show their love.
Nature's hymn, both wild and free,
Echoes in the tapestry.

Through thickets dense and shadows cast,
The creep of vines holds memories vast.
In their embrace, we find our place,
With whispered thoughts of every grace.

So linger here, where shadows lean,
And hear the secrets of the green.
In the language of the creeping lines,
Discover life where magic shines.

# The Elven Chronicles Behind the Starlit Veil

In the whisper of trees, secrets lie,
Moonlit paths where the shadows sigh.
Elven songs in the gentle breeze,
Carried softly through ancient trees.

A tapestry spun with threads of light,
In a world where day kisses night.
Glistening tides in the silver stream,
Reflecting hopes and a painter's dream.

Woven patterns of fate unspooled,
With every laugh, the darkness cooled.
Voices echo in the twilight glow,
As time drifts like a soft, pure snow.

Glimmers of stardust sprinkle the air,
As fae dance lightly without a care.
In every heart, a story swells,
Written softly in elven spells.

They speak of journeys, both ancient and new,
Of kingdoms lost and skies so blue.
For every tear that paints the soil,
Shall blossom wild in the twilight's toil.

# Entwined Writings of Light and Shadow

Ink of the heavens meets earth's embrace,
Scripted secrets in a hidden place.
Where light and shadow blend and twine,
A dance eternal, divine design.

Whispers of hope in the darkened night,
Inkling of myths that share their light.
Sketches of dreams on a parchment sky,
Where each letter dares to fly.

Fates intertwined like delicate lace,
In every heartbeat, a timeless grace.
Patterns revealed through the mystic phase,
As stars ignite in their glorious blaze.

In tangled woods where the heart does roam,
Light beckons forth to lead us home.
With every word, a promise starts,
Entwined forever—our open hearts.

## Secrets Danced Upon the Wind

On gentle zephyrs, secrets glide,
In whispers soft, the truth won't hide.
The leaves, they murmur tales of old,
In silent songs that the stars behold.

Fluttering notes like the wings of fate,
In every pause, the heart shall wait.
Echoes linger as stories take flight,
Carried swiftly into the night.

The dance of shadows, the gleam of day,
Secrets unfold in a tender play.
A tapestry woven with dreams so bright,
Guided by stars through the endless night.

From mountains high to valleys low,
Wisps of wonder, like rivers flow.
Every heartbeat, a page turned anew,
As secrets dance in the midnight blue.

## Veils of Night in the Faeries' Domain

In realms where twilight kisses the ground,
Faeries twirl, their laughter resound.
Veils of night drape soft like silk,
Enchanted whispers on vessels of milk.

Beneath the moon's silver, secrets spark,
As shadows flit through the vibrant dark.
Each flicker of light, a story is told,
Of brave little hearts, both young and old.

With every sigh of the gentle breeze,
The faeries weave magic like threads from trees.
In this domain where dreams take flight,
The stars align, painting the night.

A melody soft, like the caress of dew,
In every glimmer, the past shines through.
Veils of mystery flutter about,
As night embraces, chasing all doubt.

## The Call of the Ethereal Night

In twilight's hush, a whisper grows,
The moonlight weaves through silvered bows,
A soft enchantment fills the air,
As shadows dance without a care.

With every star, a tale is spun,
Of distant lands and battles won,
Where dreams take flight on gentle breeze,
And hearts take root in ancient trees.

The nightingale's song, a haunting plea,
Calls forth the spirits wild and free,
They gather round in silent throng,
To share the magic of their song.

A lantern glows with secrets bright,
Guiding wanderers through the night,
Each step reveals a hidden truth,
In realms untouched since fabled youth.

So heed the call of darkened skies,
For there, within the stars, it lies,
The beauty wrapped in mystic light,
Awaits your heart to take its flight.

# Bound by Starlit Sorcery

Underneath the vast expanse,
A tapestry of dreams enhance,
With every twinkle, stories rise,
Of whispered wishes and lullabies.

The cosmos hums with ancient lore,
Of hidden realms and mystical core,
As comet tails blaze across the dark,
And spark our souls with magic's spark.

A dance of fate in silver threads,
Where starlit whispers softly spread,
Binding hearts in tangled schemes,
Awakening long-forgotten dreams.

Through astral gates, our spirits soar,
Into the night where wonders pour,
With each moment, the fibers weave,
A sorcery that none can leave.

Together, we align our stars,
Amidst the glow of distant scars,
In unity, we share the night,
Forever bound in starlit light.

## Dusk's Embrace in Enchanted Realms

In twilight's arms, where shadows play,
The world transforms from bright to grey,
A secret dance beneath the trees,
Where whispers float upon the breeze.

The evening sighs, a gentle call,
As twilight softly starts to fall,
A magic stirs in dusky light,
Awakening the dreams of night.

With every star that graces sight,
A tale unfolds, a beam of light,
Of ancient spirits roaming free,
In realms of wonder, wild and glee.

As shadows stretch and colors blend,
The woven twilight knows no end,
In enchanted realms where time stands still,
With mysteries that heart can fill.

So let us wander hand in hand,
Through dusk's embrace, the dreamer's land,
And find the magic that resides,
Within the night, where hope abides.

# The Secrets Beneath the Canopy

Beneath the leaves, a world concealed,
Where whispered tales of magic yield,
In verdant shade, the secrets rest,
Awaiting hearts that seek the quest.

From tangled roots, the stories rise,
Of ancient spirits and starlit skies,
In every crack and crevice hid,
A legend lives, a wish unlid.

The sunbeams flicker through the green,
Dancing over moss, soft and serene,
While creatures small and fairies twirl,
In nature's dance, their magic unfurl.

As twilight drapes the forest low,
The whispering wind begins to blow,
It carries secrets, rich and deep,
Awakening the dreams from sleep.

So wander forth with open mind,
And leave the mundane far behind,
For in the canopy's embrace,
Lies the true magic of this place.

# Threads of Light in the Fading Day

As dusk awakens, shadows creep,
Threads of gold in twilight's sweep.
Whispers of time in colors blend,
Nature holds secrets, never to end.

The stars ignite with gentle sighs,
While gentle breezes softly rise.
In every corner, magic stirs,
Soft as the thoughts of waltzing furs.

The sky, a canvas, painted bold,
Stories of old are softly told.
A dance of fireflies by the brook,
In every flicker, a tale in a book.

With hush of night, the world transforms,
From vibrant days to quiet norms.
In the silence, dreams take flight,
As twilight fades, we embrace the night.

Life's tapestry in twilight spun,
Under the watch of the twinkling sun.
With every heartbeat, we draw near,
Threads of light dispelling fear.

# Nocturne of the Fey Beyond Time

In twilight's grip, the fey do play,
Dancing shadows, they weave and sway.
With laughter bright, they chase the stars,
In secrets held in glittering jars.

The moon, a friend, with silver beams,
Guiding hearts through slumbering dreams.
In whispers soft, they beckon near,
Casting aside all doubt and fear.

Each note, a promise, in the air,
An ancient song of love and care.
Through tangled woods where mysteries lie,
The fey of night in soft reply.

With every step, the woodland wakes,
A symphony the silence breaks.
In magical realms beyond our sight,
The fey shall keep the dreamers' night.

Through the mist, they guide the way,
In twilight realms where lost ones stay.
Countless stories must be told,
In the nocturne of the brave and bold.

# Guardians of the Dusky Realms

In shadows deep where echoes play,
Guardians rise to light the way.
With watchful eyes, they guard the night,
Keeping the darkness held in flight.

Upon the hill, their song resounds,
In ancient woods, their wisdom found.
Through ages past, their whispers call,
In unity, they stand for all.

With branches strong, the trees embrace,
As gentle winds bring forth their grace.
In every rustle, stories bloom,
Guardians shield us from the gloom.

Their spirits dance on moonlit streams,
In woven light, we chase our dreams.
With hearts entwined, we forge our fate,
In dusky realms, we celebrate.

Within their presence, courage grows,
As evening tides bring twilight's glow.
Together, we shall face the skies,
Guardians strong, we shall arise.

## Secrets Woven in Silken Spirals

In shadows cast by moon's soft glow,
Secrets whispered through the willow.
Woven tales in silken thread,
Of paths once walked, and dreams once said.

With every twist, a story spins,
Tales of loss, and love begins.
Lost in time, the echoes play,
Woven truths from yesterday.

In chambers dark where shadows lie,
The heart of magic flits and flies.
In every fold, a mystery waits,
To unlock fate at destiny's gates.

As night unfolds its velvet cloak,
The world's whispers gently stroke.
In quiet realms, enchantments rise,
Secrets twine beneath the skies.

So gather 'round, the night is young,
In stories shared, our hearts are strung.
Woven deep in silken spirals,
Secrets bloom, as time beguiles.

# Shadows Harp on Ancient Trees

In the forest where whispers sigh,
Shadows tread softly, passing by.
With leaves that dance in the breeze,
They sing the song of ancient trees.

Echoes of laughter, long since gone,
Bathe the roots in twilight's dawn.
Branches stretch like fingers old,
Each tale a secret, waiting to unfold.

Moonlight weaves through the bark so wide,
A tapestry where dreams reside.
Footfalls muffled on mossy ground,
In this sanctuary, magic is found.

A melody soft, the night's embrace,
Illuminated by time's gentle grace.
Here, beneath the wise old trees,
Shadows harp on with whispers of ease.

As stars wink down with knowing eyes,
Nature's wonders in silence rise.
Every rustle a tale to keep,
In the heart of the woods, secrets sleep.

# The Eldritch Melody of Twilight

As day succumbs to night's soft hand,
Where mystic shadows quietly stand.
The stars awaken, a flickering choir,
Singing hymns of an ancient fire.

Between the realms, a bridge appears,
Whispers carried on twilight's tears.
Notes of the cosmos weave a song,
Of wild enchantments where hearts belong.

Glimmers of hope in the dusk's embrace,
In the Eden of dreams, one finds their place.
A rhythm deep in the stillness roams,
Calling to wanderers far from their homes.

The moon a queen in her silver throne,
Guides lost spirits, never alone.
In every shadow, a story unfolds,
The eldritch melody, timeless and bold.

# Dance of the Wisp in the Dusk

In the depths where the shadows twine,
A flickering glow, a spark divine.
The will-o'-the-wisp, in whimsical jest,
Leads the way for the weary guest.

Around the ferns and through the trees,
It flutters light, a playful tease.
With trails of silver upon the ground,
In twilight's heart, mysteries abound.

It dips and sways, with laughter bright,
Crafting a path through the velvet night.
Each step a whisper, soft as a sigh,
A dance of dreams beneath the sky.

Yet caution falls on the lost and bold,
For the wayward wanderer, tales are told.
The dusk holds secrets, deep and vast,
In the dance of the wisp, shadows are cast.

# Veils of Enchantment in a Shrouded Realm

In realms where reality fades away,
Veils of enchantment hold sway.
Through mystic fog and silver mist,
Lies a secret that cannot be missed.

Whispers linger, wrapping the night,
A tapestry woven with ancient light.
Every thread a story spun,
Of battles fought and victories won.

The air hums softly with magic's breath,
In the shrouded realm where shadows rest.
Ghosts of wonders long since past,
Dance through the ages, spells to cast.

With eyes that shimmer like stars above,
The veils invite the seekers of love.
Through every corner, enchantments gleam,
In this hidden sphere, one can dream.

# Shadows that Sway with the Wind

In twilight's dance, the shadows play,
They weave through leaves, then slip away.
A whisper soft, a secret shared,
In twilight's arms, their hearts laid bare.

Beneath the boughs, the night unfolds,
The stories linger, hushed and bold.
With every rustle, dreams ignite,
While starlit paths lead hearts to flight.

The moonlight glints on paths unseen,
Where wanderers tread, their hopes serene.
With every sigh, the night replies,
In shadows deep, the courage lies.

Through murmurs low, the spirits glide,
In twilight's grace, they turn the tide.
They beckon forth, draw forth the dreams,
In swaying shadows, light redeems.

An echo calls from darkened woods,
Where magic breathes and nature broods.
In whispered tones, the wild takes flight,
As shadows sway and greet the night.

# The Guardians of the Moonlit Thicket

In thickets deep, where moonbeams glow,
The guardians stand, an ancient show.
With eyes aglow, they watch and weave,
A realm of dreams, they softly cleave.

Amongst the branches, magic swirls,
As silver light through leaves unfurls.
Gentle hearts of creatures small,
In twilight's hush, they hear the call.

With every rustle, a promise made,
In moonlit thickets, fears cascade.
These guardians bold, with secrets vast,
In woven light, weave futures past.

They guide the lost who seek to find,
A world where wonders intertwine.
With every path, a story blooms,
In tranquil thickets, solace looms.

Underneath the stars, they stand so proud,
The whispering woods, their hymn allowed.
In shadows deep, their courage gleams,
The guardians dwell where magic dreams.

## Secrets Between Woven Branches

Beneath the boughs where secrets lie,
In whispered tones, the shadows sigh.
Each woven branch a tale unfolds,
Of hidden realms and treasures untold.

The murmur of the leaves at night,
Holds dreams entwined in fading light.
A tapestry of life is spun,
In every nook, new worlds begun.

The whispered calls of creatures near,
Hold tales of hope, of love, of fear.
With every rustle, stories weave,
In tangled paths, we dare believe.

A dance of shadows, calm yet bright,
With every breath, they share their might.
In hidden glades, the heart learns pure,
That every secret holds a cure.

Between the branches, magic sways,
In gentle tones that guide our ways.
Where whispers blend in twilight's grace,
The woven branches hold their space.

# Celestial Murmurs in the Hollow

In hollows deep, where echoes dream,
The stars weave tales, a silver seam.
With cosmic whispers, time stands still,
In twilight's breath, each heart they fill.

Beneath the arch of ancient skies,
Celestial murmurs softly rise.
They paint the night in hues of gold,
As stories lost and found unfold.

The shimmering light in silence drapes,
Transcends the dusk in twinkling shapes.
Each flicker holds a life's embrace,
In cosmic dance, we find our place.

As night unfurls its velvet cloak,
The whispers blend, a timeless joke.
For every star that winks and glows,
A secret held in stillness flows.

With every heartbeat, skies align,
In hollowed silence, fates entwine.
In celestial murmurs, dreams abide,
Where hopes take flight on starlit tide.

# Chants of the Moonlit Meadows

In whispers soft, the night awakes,
The moonlit meadows softly shake.
With silver beams, the shadows dance,
Inviting dreams in twilight's trance.

Beneath the sky, the crickets sing,
To nature's voice, the heart will cling.
While fireflies twinkle, light the way,
Reflecting magic in the sway.

A breeze recalls the tales of old,
Of lovers' vows and fortunes bold.
With every breath, the meadow hums,
A lullaby to grace us from.

Let secrets weave through grasses green,
In every shadow, wonder's seen.
The moon shall guide our whispered tales,
While night unfolds its silken veils.

In silent moments, hearts confess,
The beauty held in nature's dress.
With moonlit paths that guide our feet,
In meadows fair, our souls shall meet.

# Glimmers Beneath the Foliate Canopy

In realms where sunlight softly weaves,
Through emerald leaves where magic cleaves,
The whispers of the forest sigh,
Where ancient secrets never die.

Glimmers dance on dew-kissed ferns,
As nature's heart forever churns.
The canopy, a vibrant quilt,
In every thread, a dream is built.

Each rustle speaks of journeys past,
Of fleeting moments yet to last.
With every step, the earth replies,
In harmony with waking skies.

From roots entwined, to branches high,
The stories bloom where shadows lie.
In sunlit glades, whispers grow loud,
Where hearts find peace beneath the shroud.

So linger long in nature's grace,
Embrace the magic, find your place.
For in the woods, where time stands still,
The spirit thrives, the heart's fulfilled.

# The Wisp's Guiding Light

A wisp of light upon the hill,
In darkened hours when time is still.
It flits and dances, calls the brave,
To mysteries the shadows crave.

With tender flickers, secrets share,
A gentle sigh upon the air.
In twilight's grasp, it softly weaves,
The tales of those the night believes.

Through tangled woods, the wisp will lead,
Where every heart shall find its need.
To follow light 'neath starry dome,
To guide the lost, to lead them home.

It beckons forth with playful grace,
In every corner, a familiar face.
With laughter bright, it lights the path,
For joyful hearts to share its laugh.

So trust the wisp, embrace the gleam,
In light of hope, we find our dream.
For in the night, where shadows roam,
The wisp shall always guide us home.

## Reflections on Starlit Waters

Upon the lake where stillness reigns,
The moonlight bathes like silken chains.
In mirrored depths, the stars reside,
A cosmic dance where dreams abide.

Each ripple tells a story spun,
Of journeys walked and battles won.
In tranquil echoes, hearts will soar,
As starlit whispers kiss the shore.

The night conceals a world anew,
Where hopes awaken, fears subdue.
In gentle lapping, tales unfold,
A tapestry of dreams retold.

So gaze upon the waters clear,
And let the stars draw ever near.
For in their light, the soul takes flight,
In reflections lost through endless night.

With every glance, let visions spin,
A cosmic bond that draws us in.
So raise a heart to skies so bright,
And find your peace in starlit night.

# Ethereal Silhouettes in the Dark

In shadows deep, where whispers sway,
Ethereal forms in soft ballet.
They dance with grace in midnight's hue,
Vanishing dreams, yet ever true.

A flicker here, a glimmer there,
Their presence felt, yet seen with care.
With silent steps, they glide and roam,
In lingering twilight, they find their home.

Through silver mist and starlit skies,
They weave a tale, where silence lies.
A shiver runs as they pass by,
Ethereal ghosts, who never die.

Beneath the moon, hearts beat in sync,
With every glance, they make us think.
Of worlds unseen and paths we tread,
In twilight's grasp, where dreams are led.

So come and dance, let spirits lead,
In ethereal arms, we plant a seed.
Of magic whispered in the night,
As silhouettes fade from our sight.

# Enigma of the Whispering Woods

Deep in the woods where shadows tread,
A secret whispers, softly spread.
Leaves rustle with ancient lore,
Enigmas call from the forest floor.

Moonbeams dapple on emerald boughs,
Caressing trunks as silence bows.
Voices echo in a gentle breeze,
Tales untold among the trees.

A pathway lined with emerald dreams,
Where sunlight glints and spirit beams.
Step lightly, child, and take your chance,
Amidst the woods, join in the dance.

Hidden creatures, wild and shy,
Watch over secrets as you pass by.
In the stillness, hear their call,
The woods recall, the woods enthrall.

For in this maze of ancient green,
Lies a magic yet unseen.
Embrace the enigma, let it unfold,
The whispering woods, a story retold.

# Chants of the Unseen Guardians

In realms beyond, where shadows play,
Guardians speak in a solemn sway.
Chants arise from earth and air,
Echoes of love, whispers of care.

Veiled in twilight, their voices blend,
With ancient wisdom, they transcend.
In the silence, their strength ignites,
A gentle shield that calms the nights.

They weave their magic through cosmic light,
Guiding the lost towards the right.
With every note, a promise thrives,
In unseen hands, a world survives.

So heed the calls of those unseen,
In every note, a fervent dream.
With hearts attuned to sacred sound,
The guardians watch, forever bound.

From shadows deep, they rise and sway,
Chants of the guardians light the way.
In every whisper, hear their grace,
The unseen ones, time can't erase.

# Flickering Lights in the Haunted Vale

In the haunted vale, where echoes dwell,
Flickering lights weave mystic spell.
They shimmer softly, a ghostly flame,
In the cool night air, they call your name.

Through gnarled trees and misty haze,
They dance like memories lost in a maze.
With hidden truths wrapped in their glow,
Marking the paths we dare not go.

Each flicker tells of stories past,
Of love and loss, a world amassed.
They guide the dreamers, the brave of heart,
To find the light where shadows part.

In whispers soft, their secrets spill,
Awakening courage, a hidden thrill.
For every light, a spirit shines,
In the vale of whispers where fate entwines.

So follow the glow, let it ignite,
The flickering lights in the still of night.
In haunted realms, we find the spark,
A journey bound within the dark.

# Haunting Chronicles of the Ethereal

In whispers deep where shadows creep,
The moonlight glows on secrets keep.
Lost voices call from realms unseen,
In haunted halls where time has been.

As echoes dance on silver threads,
Through shadowed paths where silence treads.
A flicker fades, a glimpse of sighs,
In midnight tales where mystery lies.

By ancient trees with twisted roots,
The stories weave in spectral shoots.
With every breath, the past reveals,
The haunting heart of fate it steals.

Beneath the stars, the specters play,
In twilight's grip, still they sway.
A chronicle of dreams and dread,
In every haunted word unsaid.

So circle 'round, dear souls that roam,
In echoes found, you find your home.
In shadows bright, let voices soar,
The ethereal cries—come, seek, explore.

# The Elysian Chamber in Twilight's Grip

In twilight's hue, the chamber glows,
With secrets clad in gentle prose.
A sanctuary of whispered dreams,
Where nothing's quite as it seems.

The luminescent night takes hold,
With tales of love and legends bold.
Each heartbeat drums in soft embrace,
In Elysium's warm, ethereal space.

Through crystal panes, the starlight streams,
A tapestry of waking dreams.
In every flicker, a hope ignites,
As shadows dance with pure delights.

The echoes swell of laughter clear,
In chambers sweet, no room for fear.
With every glance, the night unfolds,
In warmth of light, its truth enfolds.

As twilight wraps the world in grace,
The chamber holds a sacred place.
In tranquil tones, let hearts begin,
To feel the magic dwelling in.

# A Tapestry of Shadows Wrought in Light

Within the weave of night and day,
A tapestry where shadows play.
With colors bright and tones so deep,
In threads of time, the secrets keep.

Each lesson learned, a stitch is sewn,
In twilight's brush, the truth is grown.
For every shadow, light bestows,
A dance of fate that gently flows.

Among the hues of dusk and dawn,
The fabric stirs, life's magic drawn.
In every corner, echoes trace,
A whispered touch, a fleeting grace.

So weave your hopes with dreams beyond,
In every thread, a bond, a bond.
With light and shadow, hands shall meet,
A wondrous world where hearts compete.

Embrace the dance of every shade,
In this grand tapestry that's made.
For shadows wrought in light will gleam,
And weave the fabric of our dream.

# Murmurs of the Fey on Silent Wings

As dusk descends with gentle sighs,
The Fey alight 'neath velvet skies.
With laughter soft, in whispers sweet,
They paint the night—our souls to greet.

On silent wings, they flit and play,
In twilight's glow, they find their way.
With every flicker, magic swells,
As nature's secrets dance in spells.

In glades where silver shadows thrive,
The fey expound the dreams alive.
Each murmur holds a world untold,
In tender truths, our hearts enfold.

With shimmering lights, they twine and drift,
Their ways a gift, a precious gift.
In every verse, a summoning call,
To join their dance beneath the fall.

So linger not in waking hours,
For magic blooms in blooming flowers.
The Fey invite with open grace,
To this enchanted, timeless place.

# Dance of the Nightshade Spirits

In shadows cast by moonlit grace,
The nightshade spirits twirl and trace,
With whispers soft as silken threads,
They weave their dance where silence treads.

Around the trees, a spectral glow,
They spin and glide, the cool winds blow,
Each movement holds a tale untold,
In the twilight, dreams unfold.

They beckon souls from far and wide,
To join their revels, side by side,
A fleeting chance to lose one's care,
In this enchanted, breathless air.

With petals dark and shimmering eyes,
They mark the end where magic lies,
In circles drawn where shadows blend,
The nightshade dance shall never end.

As dawn's first light begins to rise,
The spirits fade, a soft goodbye,
Yet linger still is their sweet song,
In hearts where nightshade spirits throng.

# Sylvan Veils and Hidden Paths

Through sylvan veils where secrets hide,
The ancient woods, a whispered guide,
With roots entwined in dreams of old,
Their stories wait for hearts so bold.

Along the paths where shadows creep,
The echoes of the past run deep,
In every rustle, in every sigh,
The spirits of the forest lie.

Beneath the boughs, the twilight glows,
And in the stillness, magic flows,
Each winding trail a chance to roam,
To find the place we call our home.

With every step, enchantments weave,
A tapestry of tales to leave,
In whispers soft and gentle light,
We journey onward through the night.

The sylvan paths, forever drawn,
To lead us forth from dusk till dawn,
In hidden realms where dreams ignite,
We wander on, a pure delight.

# The Lure of the Starlit Hollow

In starlit hollow, dreams take flight,
Where whispers dance in soft moonlight,
A place where wishes weave their thread,
And hearts are filled with words unsaid.

Beneath the arch of glowing skies,
The magic twinkles, softly sighs,
Each glow a promise, bright and clear,
To chase away the shadowed fear.

With silver streams and faerie tune,
The hollow sings beneath the moon,
A beckoning to those who roam,
To find within its depths a home.

In laughter shared and stories spun,
Where every heart can be as one,
We gather close, 'neath stars so bold,
In this sweet haven, dreams unfold.

When dawn arrives, and shadows wane,
We'll carry forth the starlit gain,
A treasure held, forever bright,
The lure of love, our guiding light.

## Realm of Shimmering Whispers

In the realm where whispers gleam,
Shimmering like a waking dream,
Each secret held in tender grace,
A timeless dance in endless space.

With laughter wrapped in golden threads,
The echoes of the past still spread,
Through twilight meadows where they play,
Unfolding tales from yesterday.

Here in the hush, desires bloom,
Fleeting shadows in the gloom,
A glimpse of hope in every sigh,
Where dreams and wishes dare to fly.

Embrace the light that softly calls,
Beyond the veils, where magic falls,
In every heartbeat, life persists,
In shimmering whispers, love exists.

As twilight wanes and night draws near,
The realm persists, forever dear,
In every whisper, glint, and spark,
In shimmering realms, we leave our mark.

# Soft Whispers Among the Thorned Roses

In gardens where the shadows creep,
The roses keep their secrets deep.
With fragrant sighs and petals bright,
They whisper tales beneath the night.

A breeze that dances through the thorns,
Brings echoes of the softest scorns.
In twilight's glow, their colors gleam,
At dusk they weave a silent dream.

Amongst the blooms, a haunting song,
Of love and loss that feels so wrong.
The thorns may prick, the petals sigh,
But in their heart, the spirits lie.

A flicker of light, a shadow cast,
In every bloom, a memory vast.
With whispered joys and muted fears,
The roses tell of bygone years.

As moonlight bathes the sleeping glade,
The secret paths through dreams are laid.
In softest whispers, hope arises,
Among the roses, truth comprises.

# Echoing Festivals of the Gloom

In a grove where the shadows play,
The lanterns flicker, dreams betray.
Amidst the dance of cloaked delight,
The night unveils its ghostly light.

The drums thump low, a heartbeat's cry,
As spirits rise and shadows sigh.
With every laugh and every tear,
The echoes weave through dusk and fear.

They gather 'round the ancient tree,
In whispered tones of memory.
Each face aglow with haunting cheer,
Yet hidden lies a tale of fear.

A feast of sorrow, joys unfurl,
As goblets raise in shadowed whirl.
The revelers caught in whispered doom,
Still celebrate in the gathering gloom.

Yet as the night begins to fade,
The laughter mingles, ghosts invade.
In every cheer, a solemn tune,
Echoing festivals beneath the moon.

# The Enchanted Bothy of Lost Secrets

A cabin stands where shadows dwell,
With whispers woven by a spell.
The hearth still glows with embers rare,
Its walls are steeped in ancient air.

Within those beams, the stories hide,
Of wanderers and time defied.
With creaking boards and sighing beams,
It holds the weight of fractured dreams.

Through dusty windows, fades the light,
Yet flickers hope in the deepening night.
A flick of flame, a shadowed ghost,
Will sing the dreams that matter most.

The bothy speaks in riddles spun,
Of battles lost and victories won.
Each corner hides a tale untold,
In echoes soft, the past unfolds.

Amongst the moss and tangled vines,
The magic waits, the fate entwines.
In enchanted air, the heart may find,
The secrets lost to time's cruel bind.

## Melodies of the Twilight Celts

When day surrenders to the night,
The melodies take wing in flight.
With harps that hum and voices clear,
The twilight sings so sweet and near.

A gathering 'neath the ancient oaks,
Where laughter blooms and wisdom chokes.
In every note, a tale of old,
Of myths and legends softly told.

With dances light as whispered air,
The Celts will twirl without a care.
With every step, the earth will sway,
In twilight's grace, they lose their way.

The stars above begin to gleam,
While shadows weave a silver dream.
In harmony, their hearts align,
As moonbeams kiss the darkened vine.

With every song, the shadows blend,
In melodies that never end.
The twilight Celts, in joyous trance,
Will fill the night with sacred dance.

# Whispers in the Twilight Grove

In twilight's grasp, where shadows play,
The whispers dance beneath the sway,
Of ancient trees with secrets old,
In their embrace, the tales unfold.

A breeze will carry stories deep,
Of dreams once lost, now wake from sleep,
With every rustle, hearts will sigh,
And stars above begin to cry.

The moonlight filters through the leaves,
Like silver threads, it softly weaves,
A tapestry of night and song,
That lingers sweet, where we belong.

Beneath the sky, so vast and bright,
The grove holds secrets, pure delight,
For every sound, a tale revealed,
In twilight's hush, our fate is sealed.

So come, dear friend, and take your share,
Of magic spun with gentle care,
In whispers soft, we find our ways,
In twilight's grove, we'll spend our days.

## Shadows Dance on Silver Wings

Upon the breeze, the shadows glide,
With silver wings, they gracefully hide,
In twilight's charm, they weave their fate,
A dance of dusk, where dreams await.

The forest sighs, a soft embrace,
As time slows down in this sacred space,
With every twirl, a secret spun,
In enchanted realms, we are but one.

Luminous glimmers chase the night,
In patterns woven with pure delight,
The whispers echo through the trees,
Among the shadows, a gentle breeze.

The stars above shine bright and keen,
In this moment, pure and serene,
With shadows dancing, hearts entwine,
In silver hues, our souls align.

So let us wander, hand in hand,
Through moonlit paths, across the land,
For in this dance, we find our song,
And with the shadows, we belong.

## The Enchantment of Gloomy Glades

In gloomy glades where mist doth cling,
The whispers of the shadows sing,
A haunting melody of night,
That beckons forth with soft delight.

The ancient oaks, with boughs stretched wide,
Embrace the gloom with arms of pride,
Each leaf a tale, a whispered fate,
In silent glades where dreams await.

The air is thick with magic's trace,
A gentle pulse, a warm embrace,
For every step on mossy floor,
Unravel secrets, evermore.

Moonlight spills like silver rain,
Upon the glades that hold our pain,
Yet in the dark, the beauty glows,
In shadows deep, true wonder flows.

So tread with care through edged light,
And hold the magic of the night,
For in these glades, our hearts shall soar,
And find the peace we seek, once more.

# Secrets of the Moonlit Thicket

In thickets deep, where shadows sleep,
The moonlight casts a subtle sweep,
With silver beams on leaves so bright,
It holds the secrets of the night.

A rustling sound, a whispered word,
In every rustle, dreams are stirred,
The thicket hums with ancient lore,
Of magic lost and found once more.

The pathways twist in gentle bends,
Where time stands still and magic mends,
With every step, the night unfolds,
A tapestry of dreams and golds.

In silence shared, we walk as one,
Beneath the gaze of stars undone,
For in the thicket, hearts will bloom,
As secrets dance in soft perfume.

So linger near, and breathe it in,
The thicket's charm, where we begin,
For every secret softly spun,
Holds the promise of dreams begun.

# Tales from the Sylvan Shadows

In the woods where whispers sigh,
Shadows dance as night birds fly.
Beneath the boughs where secrets dwell,
Nature spins her timeless spell.

Elusive light through leaves does weave,
In hushed tones, the ancient trees grieve.
Creatures stir in twilight's grace,
Awaiting fate in this hidden place.

Moonlight glimmers on a stream,
Reflecting dreams, a fleeting beam.
Forgotten paths where fairies tread,
Guide lost souls to realms long dead.

Whispers linger, stories old,
In each heartbeat, wonders unfold.
Every shadow, a tale unknown,
In the sylvan depths, magic is grown.

So pause awhile, let breath catch tight,
In the embrace of the coming night.
For in these woods, beyond the sight,
Lies the truth, shrouded in light.

# Enigmas of the Midnight Sylph

Underneath the midnight haze,
A sylph weaves through moonlit maze.
With laughter soft as silken threads,
She twirls where only magic spreads.

A riddle borne upon the breeze,
Breaking hearts, yet setting free,
Each glance a spark, each breath a chance,
In twilight's clasp, they join the dance.

Veiled in shadows, secrets lie,
Glimmers of color flash and fly.
Her whispers echo, faint yet clear,
Drawing lost dreams ever near.

In emerald glades where roses bloom,
She spins chaos, dances gloom.
With each fleeting sigh, hearts align,
In this embrace, the worlds entwine.

So come, ye wanderers, hear her call,
In the depths of night, you too may fall.
Tread lightly here, where dreams entwine,
With the midnight sylph, in lost design.

## In the Heart of the Verdant Night

In the heart of night so deep,
Where shadows play and secrets seep,
The leaves converse in murmured song,
And every breeze feels ancient, strong.

Moonlight spills on mossy ground,
With whispers lost, yet still profound.
A flicker of wings, the hush of dusk,
In the cool embrace of earth's own husk.

Awake are spirits, both wild and free,
Guardians of night, in harmony.
Guiding the dreamers with tender grace,
Within the wild, they find their place.

Time drifts gently, rivers flow,
In twilight's grasp, soft hearts will glow.
For every soul with stars above,
Finds solace here, finds radiant love.

So wander forth, let wonder lead,
In this verdant night, plant each seed.
For in the dark, a spark ignites,
And dreams shall bloom in endless nights.

## The Sylph's Lament in Emerald Depths

Deep beneath the emerald swell,
The sylph's soft sigh began to dwell.
A melody of heart's despair,
In shadowed woods, she spun her care.

With each note, the forest wept,
For dreams once held, now tightly kept.
Echoes of laughter in whispers lost,
A haunting tune of love's great cost.

Her wings like twilight, fragile, light,
Adrift in darkness, amid the night.
She weaves her tale in sorrow's bind,
A bittersweet song for hearts confined.

In emerald depths, the spirits lie,
Guardians of whispers, as echoes die.
They dance in silence, shadows blend,
Each sylph's lament, a heart to mend.

Yet hope remains in each sigh's breath,
A promise whispered beyond the death.
For every loss, a love reborn,
In the sylph's lament, new dreams adorn.

# Whispers in the Twilight Grove

In twilight's embrace, the secrets sigh,
As leaves dance softly, beneath the sky.
Murmurs of magic, in the air they weave,
Echoing dreams that no hearts perceive.

With every rustle, a tale unfolds,
Of heroes and legends, of treasures untold.
The twilight grove holds the world's gentle breath,
Where shadows and light weave the fabric of death.

A flickering glow from the fireflies' flight,
Guides lost souls home through the shroud of night.
In the hush of the forest, all doubts disappear,
As whispers of wonder drench the night clear.

Each glimmering star, a guardian bright,
Watches o'er secrets in the soft velvet night.
Roots intertwine stories of those long gone,
While the twilight grove sings its ancient song.

So linger a moment, let your heart soar,
In whispers of twilight, there's so much in store.
For in this still haven, all will be revealed,
The magic of night, forever concealed.

# Shadows Beneath the Moonlit Canopy


Beneath the moon's gaze, where shadows dance,
The secrets of night spark a curious glance.
Starlight weaves tales over silver leaves,
Whispers of fables the darkness believes.

A fleeting breeze stirs the ancient trees,
Carrying stories that wander with ease.
In the heart of the night, dreams blend and collide,
As the moonlit canopy cradles the tide.

Lost in the twilight, where visions entwine,
A spell of enchantment begins to align.
Echoes of laughter drift through the air,
As shadows awaken, weaving magic rare.

Glimmers of silver ignite every path,
Lead wanderers softly, away from the wrath.
Where beauty and mystery embrace like a friend,
Shadows beneath the moonlit night's end.

So tiptoe with care, hear the nightbirds' song,
For in the stillness, you truly belong.
The magic of shadows, forever shall muse,
In realms of the night, where dreams dare to fuse.

# Secrets of the Enchanted Glade

In the heart of the woods lies a glade so grand,
Where whispers of magic meet a gentle hand.
A tapestry woven, with threads of pure light,
In secrets enchanted, day melds into night.

The flowers bloom bright, with colors that sing,
While faeries and sprites gather round in a ring.
A flicker of laughter ignites every breath,
In the enchanted glade, where joy conquers death.

Glimmers of hope dance on the soft, dewy grass,
Where every moment holds treasures that pass.
Breathe deep the fragrance of magic in air,
For secrets of dreams linger everywhere.

The ancient oak watches with wisdom untold,
Guarding the stories that never grow old.
In the hush of the glade, let your wishes take flight,
For magic awakens beneath the starlit night.

So wander with purpose, let your spirit roam,
In the embrace of the glade, you'll find your true home.
For in every secret, a new world begins,
In the heart of the glade, where adventure spins.

# Echoes of Forgotten Realms

In realms of the past, where echoes reside,
Whispers of ages flow like a tide.
Each corner is woven with shadows of yore,
As dreams paint the air with legends in store.

Beyond every portal, adventures await,
Through time-worn pathways, we beckon fate.
With each step we take, a new chapter gleams,
In echoes of worlds born from midnight dreams.

The stars bear witness to stories retold,
Of friendships forged deep, courageous and bold.
In lingering shadows, the spirits align,
To guide wandering hearts 'neath the celestial design.

In the depths of the night, old melodies play,
As whispers of magic drift slowly away.
Lost realms awaken, their mysteries spun,
In echoes of shadows, our journeys begun.

So listen intently for the call that you hear,
In echoes of realms, let go of your fear.
For every adventure belongs to the bold,
In the tapestry woven, forever unfold.

## The Fae's Forgotten Whispering Song

In the glade where shadows play,
Echoes of laughter drift away,
A tune once bright, now dimmed by time,
Whispers lost, in the forest's rhyme.

Moonlight dances on silver streams,
Carrying secrets of ancient dreams,
Fae flit softly on glittering wings,
Unseen guardians of mystic things.

Songs of old, with notes of gold,
Woven in tales that once were told,
The heart of the woods still longs to hear,
The fae's sweet song, both far and near.

Yet moments fade like the morning dew,
And silence reigns where magic grew,
But in the breeze, if you listen close,
You'll hear the song that you want the most.

A melody lost, a wish concealed,
In twilight's glow, it's slowly revealed,
The fae's forgotten whispering song,
In every sigh, where we belong.

## Twilight's Embrace in the Sylvan Realm

Beneath the boughs of ancient trees,
A hush falls gently on the breeze,
Twilight gathers, soft and sweet,
In the sylvan realm where shadows meet.

Fingers of gold, the sun retreats,
As night unveils her starry sheets,
Whispers of magic in the air,
A promise held in twilight's care.

The moon climbs high in velvet skies,
Casting spells where the owl flies,
Secrets dance on silken threads,
In a world where starlit dreams are bred.

Silhouettes of ferns, aglow with light,
Invoke enchantments in the night,
In the embrace of shadows deep,
The sylvan heart begins to leap.

Here in stillness, time does bend,
Beneath the trees, our spirits blend,
With twilight's grace, we lose our fears,
In the magical realm of whispered years.

# The Melancholy of Faerie Dreams

In moonlit glens where shadows sigh,
The fae weave dreams that flit and fly,
But dreams can turn to wistful tears,
In the heart of night, where hope appears.

Upon the moss, the softest bed,
Each whispered wish, so tenderly said,
Yet echoes linger of joy once bold,
In a world where stories often unfold.

Glimmers of light, like starlit dust,
Paint every corner with gentle trust,
But melancholy whispers in the breeze,
Stirring the leaves of ancient trees.

Caught in the web of dreams forlorn,
The fae sing songs of love reborn,
Where every breath holds a twinge of pain,
In the beauty of loss, we dance again.

So let the dusk embrace our fears,
As twilight fades, and so do years,
In the garden of dreams, where faeries roam,
We find the strength to call our heart home.

# The Enigma of Phosphorescent Trails

In the depths of night, where wonders gleam,
Phosphorescent trails weave a dream,
A sparkling path through the murk and mist,
Guiding the heart, with a gentle twist.

With each step taken, the secrets unfold,
Stories of magic, both new and old,
Drawing the wanderer into the glade,
Where whispers of enchantment shall never fade.

Light dances playfully on dew-kissed ferns,
Revealing the world in shimmering turns,
The enigma calls with a beckoning hand,
Leading you forth to a timeless land.

But beware the shadows that linger near,
For not all trails bring comfort or cheer,
The phosphorescent glow, so bright and bold,
Hides truths unspoken, mysteries untold.

Follow the light where the fae may tread,
In the echoes of dusk, let your spirit be led,
For in every shimmer, a story ignites,
In the enigma of phosphorescent nights.

# Phantoms in the Gathered Dusk

In twilight's embrace, shadows dance slow,
Phantoms awaken, where soft breezes blow.
Whispers of secrets in fading light,
Echo through silence, vanish from sight.

Cloaked figures roam, with hearts full of dreams,
Threads of lost stories unwind at the seams.
The air hushed and heavy, time holds its breath,
In the gathering dusk, all flirt with death.

Glimmers of laughter blend in the dark,
As memories tremble, igniting the spark.
In corners forgotten, they flicker and glow,
The past intertwines with the ghosts that we know.

Chasing the night with a lantern in hand,
Seeking the tales we don't understand.
Though shadows may linger, hope weaves its thread,
In the dance of phantoms, we learn to be led.

# Lanterns Among the Misted Thorns

In a garden wrapped in mist's gentle shroud,
Lanterns flicker softly, a luminous crowd.
Among twisted thorns, their light has begun,
Guiding lost wanderers, one by one.

Petals drip dew, like tears from the night,
Each lantern's glow casting magical light.
Whispers entwined with the rustling leaves,
Bringing to life tales that the heart weaves.

Through shadows they wander, with hope held aloft,
Seeking the warmth that nature has soft.
With thorns just a watchman, the path is made clear,
For those who are lost, the lanterns draw near.

Secrets awaken beneath the moon's gaze,
In the misty thicket where magic will blaze.
Here, among thorns, love's embers ignite,
Lanterns glow brighter, dispelling the night.

## Memories of the Whispering Grove

In the heart of the grove where the ancients reside,
Memories linger, in shadows they bide.
The whispers of ages weave in the air,
Stories of joy and unfathomable despair.

Leaves rustle gently in soft, secret songs,
Echoing stories of righting of wrongs.
Trees bear the weight of each tale they hold,
In the grove's gentle hush, all is retold.

The essence of laughter, the warmth of a tear,
Resides in each branch, draws the lost near.
In silence they gather, these fragments of time,
Bound in the fabric of rhythm and rhyme.

Here, under starlight, the past comes alive,
Memories whisper and in shadows they thrive.
Amongst tangled roots and the moonlight's grace,
The grove reveals secrets in this sacred space.

# Luminescent Glades of Forgotten Tales

In glades where the whispers of fairies might dwell,
Luminescent glimmers enchant and compel.
Forgotten tales linger in twilight's soft glow,
Casting their magic on all that we know.

The canopy shimmers with starlit delight,
As echoes of stories take wing in the night.
Branches entwined like fingers of fate,
Guide wayward travelers to forgotten gate.

Within every shadow, a story awaits,
Of lovers and legends, long kept by the fates.
Fables unfold in the cool evening air,
As glades come alive with sweet dreams everywhere.

Through luminous paths where the wild things roam,
The heart finds its compass, leads the lost home.
Here in the glades, where the echoes prevail,
The whispers of magic share forgotten tales.

# The Haunting Lullaby of Ancient Trees

In the forest deep, where shadows play,
Whispers of time echo through the day.
Branches entwined, like fingers hold tight,
Guardians of secrets, shrouded in night.

Leaves softly rustle, a melodic sigh,
As the stars above begin to pry.
Stories unfold in the cool evening air,
Nature's own ballad, beyond compare.

Roots stretch below, a network of dreams,
Caught in the stillness, where silence seems.
Cloaked in mystery, the ancients sigh,
Lullabies sung as the ages fly.

Moss-covered stones and the sighing pines,
Time weaves a tapestry, ancient designs.
In dappled sunlight, shadows do weave,
Magic lives on in those who believe.

So linger a while, let your heart roam,
In the haunting lullaby, you'll find your home.
With every breath, let the stories weave,
In the arms of the trees, learn to believe.

# A Symphony of Ethereal Flickers

In twilight's glow, a dance begins,
Flickers of light where the magic spins.
Fairy wings flutter, a shimmering hue,
Painting the world in ethereal blue.

Melodies drift on a soft evening breeze,
Whispers of wonders wrap round the trees.
As laughter and joy in the air intertwine,
The night is alive with a spark divine.

Crickets keep time with a starlit song,
In the heart of the night, where dreams belong.
Each pulse of the glow, a sentient spark,
Guiding the wanderer through the dark.

Through glades and paths, the magic will call,
In the flickering light, we rise, we fall.
Hearts beating softly, in time with the night,
Lost in the symphony, out of our sight.

So let your spirit take flight and soar,
With ethereal flickers, forever explore.
In the world woven thin, beneath the star's gleam,
Join in the dance of every dream.

## Nightfall's Embrace in Fae Meanders

As dusk paints the sky with a velvet brush,
The fae come alive in the twilight hush.
Through moonlit glades, they twirl and spin,
Whispers of magic where dreams begin.

Beneath ancient oaks, in shadows they play,
With laughter that echoes, leading astray.
A symphony crafted from leaves and from light,
Nightfall's embrace cloaks the magical night.

Stars twinkle bright, like secrets confessed,
In the realm of the fae, where all are blessed.
A tapestry woven with starlight and glee,
Mysteries linger in every tree.

Through enchanted paths that twist and turn,
Hearts full of wonder and lessons to learn.
With every step, the night softly sighs,
In fae meanders, where magic lies.

So lose yourself in the twilight's caress,
In nightfall's embrace, find your true quest.
Each shadow a story, each breeze a new song,
In the fae's gentle grip, forever belong.

# The Darkling Revelry


In the depths of night, where shadows grow,
A revelry stirs, in the moon's soft glow.
Masked in the twilight, secrets unwind,
The darkling spirits leave daylight behind.

Footsteps echo, on frost-kissed grass,
With whispers and laughter, a daring pass.
Gathered in circles, in time's gentle flow,
The dance of the ages, a mystical show.

Glimmers of mischief in every glance,
Wily and bold, they invite you to dance.
With waltzes of starlight, and twirls of delight,
The night stretches on, enveloping tight.

From shadows they spring, with flamboyant grace,
Twisting and turning, no time to waste.
The darkling's allure, both wild and free,
In the heart of the night, they beckon thee.

So join in the revel, let go of your fears,
In the dance of the dark, as the dawn appears.
With laughter and joy, in the moon's bright dream,
The darkling revelry, a shimmering stream.

# Echoes of the Sylvan Shadows

In the depths where shadows dwell,
Whispers spin a secret spell.
Leaves shimmer with a twilight gleam,
Life unfolds like a forgotten dream.

Through the branches, voices sing,
Songs of joy and blossoming spring.
Softly rustles the ancient trees,
Guardians of a time that frees.

Moonlit paths invite us near,
Carrying stories for those who hear.
Footsteps trace a winding way,
Guided by the silver ray.

In the heart of sylvan hush,
Echoes linger, soft as brush.
Nature's cradle, warm and wide,
Welcomes souls who seek to bide.

With every glimpse of dawn's embrace,
Shadows dance in a timeless space.
Their laughter floats on crystal air,
Binding earth with spirits rare.

# Midnight Lament of the Woodland Spirits

When the clock strikes the midnight hour,
Whispers bloom, in moonlight's power.
A haunting call from deep within,
The woodland spirits weave their sin.

In the glades where lost dreams play,
Echoes of sorrow softly sway.
Each flicker of a firefly's glow,
Carries tales of long ago.

Silvery mists wrap the trees tight,
Veiling shadows from the light.
A symphony of wilted sighs,
Haunts the dusk as daylight dies.

With every rustle, memories flood,
Like gentle waves against the wood.
Grief hangs heavy on the breeze,
A lingering weight beneath the leaves.

In every breeze that whispers low,
Lamenting hearts take to the flow.
From branches high to roots below,
The woodland spirits quietly know.

# Veils of Mist in Dreaming Hollows

In the hollows where dreams reside,
Veils of mist in silence glide.
Softly nestled in the earth,
Whispering secrets of rebirth.

Through the fog, a silhouette stands,
Shaped by magic, woven strands.
Echoes linger of adventures bold,
Tales of wonders yet untold.

Each dawn breaks like a lover's sigh,
Painting the canvas of the sky.
Misty visions cascade and swirl,
In moonlit arms they dance and twirl.

Dreams cascade like gentle streams,
Flowing softly into our dreams.
With each heartbeat, the shadows weave,
Threads of night that never leave.

In the heart of dreaming time,
Veils enfold, whispering rhyme.
Hollows echo with laughter bright,
Holding magic in its light.

# Lullabies from the Hidden Glens

In the glens where shadows play,
Lullabies drift at end of day.
Soft and sweet, they cradle night,
Hushing the world till morning light.

Nature's choir, a gentle hum,
Brought to life by a distant drum.
Every note a tender bond,
Wrapping dreams in a verdant fond.

Leaves rustle in a soothing breeze,
Singing secrets among the trees.
From the brook, a soft refrain,
Cascading like gentle rain.

Twilight dances in golden hues,
Echoes fade into dusk's blues.
Moonbeams cast their silver lace,
Lullabies breathe in this embrace.

Here beneath the starry dome,
Every glen becomes a home.
In nature's arms, the weary rest,
Finding solace, truly blessed.

# Reverie of the Enchanted Shadows

In twilight's grasp, where whispers dwell,
A tapestry of dreams begins to swell.
With moonlit threads and starlit seams,
The shadows weave the fabric of dreams.

Beneath the boughs where secrets lie,
The evening sighs, a gentle cry.
Through gossamer paths, the echoes soar,
Inviting hearts to explore once more.

As twilight fades to deep midnight,
The shadows dance in shimmering light.
With every twirl, the magic grows,
In this realm where enchantment flows.

A spell is cast on hearts so pure,
In shadows deep, we find the cure.
A fleeting glimpse of something bright,
A reverie held through the night.

So linger here, a moment's grace,
Among the shadows, find your place.
In dreams where dusk and dawn unite,
The heart takes wing, ready for flight.

# The Ethereal Skirmish Under Starlit Canopies

Beneath the arch of ancient trees,
Where whispers stir in zephyr's breeze,
Two forces clash in silent grace,
An ethereal dance in time and space.

Fairies twirl with glimmering light,
While sprites engage in playful flight.
The stars observe with watchful eyes,
As dreams and wonders intertwine and rise.

A shimmer of wings, a flash of glow,
Through starlit lanes where magic flows.
Each flicker speaks of rivalry,
In cosmic realms of mystery.

Through shadowed bends and hidden glades,
The echoes linger, never fades.
A symphony of joy and plight,
The skirmish swirls 'neath silver light.

As dawn approaches, battles cease,
The night surrenders, granting peace.
With gentle sigh, the world awakes,
To the tales a new day makes.

# Flickers of Lost Dreams in the Night

In the hush of night, a whisper calls,
As echoes bounce off ancient walls.
Flickers of dreams that slipped away,
Dance in the dusk where shadows play.

A phantom touch, a fleeting sight,
Reminds the heart of love's pure light.
In the corners where silence dwells,
Lost dreams linger, casting spells.

Through silvered veils of moonlit rays,
Memories twine in forgotten ways.
Each sigh reveals a hidden lore,
Of dreams once held, now sought once more.

These flickers hold a soft embrace,
A promise of time and sacred space.
Through weary eyes, we glimpse the past,
In fleeting moments that leave us aghast.

So gather close, let memories flow,
In the darkest nights, let your heart know.
For every flicker, a tale unfolds,
Of dreams once bright, now softly told.

# Nymphs' Secrets Carried by the Breeze

In meadows lush, where wildflowers bloom,
Nymphs gather 'neath the silver moon.
With laughter light and voices sweet,
They weave the threads where dreams do meet.

Carried by winds, their secrets glide,
In whispered tones, where spirits bide.
Each rustling leaf, a tale unfurls,
Of ancient wisdom, the heart of worlds.

They dance on streams, their joy revealed,
In every ripple, magic sealed.
Through twilight's gaze, they gracefully glide,
Bringing solace to those who confide.

With every breeze, a legacy flows,
Nurturing hopes that gently grows.
In their embrace, we all belong,
To nature's heart, a timeless song.

So heed the whispers, let them in,
As nymphs might urge, new journeys begin.
With open hearts, embrace the breeze,
Unraveling secrets that nature leaves.

# Shadows Resting on Leafy Beds

In a whispering grove where the sunlight fades,
Shadows settle softly on leafy beds.
The secrets of nature in silence cascade,
Awaiting the dreams that the night gently spreads.

Crickets sing lullabies beneath the moon's glow,
While fireflies flicker in delicate flight.
The forest awakens, a soft, gentle show,
As shadows and dreams take their dance in the night.

Underneath branches where stillness resides,
Wise owls keep watch with their vigilant eyes.
Mysteries woven where darkness abides,
Every whisper of leaf carries thoughts to the skies.

Amongst ancient trees, the deep shadows yawn,
Embracing the stillness like a warm coat.
With the dawn approaching, the remnants are drawn,
As shadows retreat and the sunlight takes note.

So here in this haven where peace gently lies,
Let your mind wander through stirring delight.
For here in the shadows, the heart never dies,
And dreams find their rest in the cloak of the night.

## The Faerie's Secret Path of Shadows


In twilight's embrace where the faeries play,
A path made of shadows begins to unwind.
With whispers of magic that lead them away,
To realms unexplored, where the heart is aligned.

Dancing on petals, their laughter ignites,
Glimmers of silver reflect in the air.
They twirl amongst blossoms in soft, gentle nights,
While shadows weave tales, with grace beyond compare.

This secretive path, paved in starlit dreams,
Beneath boughs entwined with the velvet of dusk.
Guides wandering souls as the moon gently beams,
To secrets unveiled in the night's fragrant husk.

Through thickets of thyme, where the nightingale sings,
These faeries, so graceful, allure the pure heart.
In corners of whispers, enchantment still clings,
Where shadows together shall never depart.

So follow the faeries, their path will entice;
For under the cover of starlight's soft hue,
Adventures await, like a well-hidden vice,
In the faerie's secret, the heart starts anew.

## Beneath the Glistening Boughs of Enchantment

Beneath the glistening boughs, a wonder unfolds,
Where secrets lie wrapped in the moon's silvery thread.
Whispers of magic, like stories retold,
Awaken the senses, and dreams lie ahead.

In dappled light dancing through leaves overhead,
The air hums with laughter, a child's playful mirth.
Here where the ancients and nature have tread,
The heart finds a rhythm of joy and rebirth.

Moss carpets the ground, a soft pillow of green,
As shadows embrace, weaving stories anew.
In the hush of the forest, a soft, serene sheen,
Awaits those who venture, both brave and true.

With each gentle breath, the world fades away,
Each creature attuned to the song of the night.
In the dance of the fireflies, magic will sway,
Illuminating paths where the heart takes its flight.

So linger a moment, let wonder take hold,
For beneath ancient boughs, enchantment is spun.
With stories and dreams that through ages were told,
In the heart of the forest, our journey's begun.

## The Dance of Dusk's Embrace

As daylight surrenders to twilight's soft kiss,
The world holds its breath in the serene glow.
The dance of dusk rises, an ephemeral bliss,
Where shadows and whispers commence their soft flow.

Under the canvas of swirling deep hues,
The stars start to twinkle, the moon comes alive.
Filling the air with a calmness to choose,
In the dance of the evening, our spirits revive.

Petals of night bloom in fragrant release,
While owls call to one another, their echo resounds.
Every glance is a treasure, a moment of peace,
As creatures of night seek the magic that surrounds.

The rustling of leaves, a soft lullaby's breath,
Carried on whispers, a love song anew.
In dusk's gentle grasp, there's no shadow of death,
For the dance of this moment, forever rings true.

So cherish the dusk, let it cradle your heart;
In its soft, mellow embrace, find solace and grace.
For every end births a newness, a start,
In the dance of dusk's arms, we all find our place.

www.ingramcontent.com/pod-product-compliance
Ingram Content Group UK Ltd.
Pitfield, Milton Keynes, MK11 3LW, UK
UKHW021320230125

4262UKWH00004B/29